WHO GIVES A SH*T

Peter Davidson

WHO GIVES A SH*T

Peter Davidson

SWEET MEMORIES PUBLISHING

A Division of Sweet Memories, Inc.

sweetmemories@mchsi.com

If you purchased this book without a cover, you should be aware that this book is stolen property. It was reported "unsold and destroyed" to the publisher and neither the author nor the publisher has received any payment for this "stripped book."

Copyright © 2013 by Peter Davidson

All rights reserved. No part of this book may be used or reproduced in whole or part or transmitted in any form or by any means, electronic or mechanical, without permission from the publisher except for a reviewer who wishes to use brief quotations for a review in newspapers, magazines, or other form of broadcast. For information address Sweet Memories Publishing, Sweet Memories, Inc., P.O. Box 497, Arnolds Park, IA 51331-0497.

ISBN: 978-0-9762718-6-4
Library of Congress Control Number: 2013942074
First Printing, August, 2013

Published by Sweet Memories Publishing
A division of Sweet Memories, Inc.
P.O. Box 497
Arnolds Park, IA 51331-0497

PRINTED IN THE UNITED STATES OF AMERICA

10 9 8 7 6 5 4 3 2 1

Acknowledgements

Editor: Beterzone Wordright Services

Graphic Design: Jean Tennant

Proofreader: B. Peterson

Table of Contents

TELLING IT LIKE IT IS

FIRST TEN THINGS NOBODY GIVES A SHIT ABOUT
    Rejection 3
    Bubba Day 3
    Doorbuster 4
    Blacklisted 4
    HUH? 5
    Long Liver 6
    Breaking News 6
    How Ya Doin'? 7
    Socialite Book 8
    Holiday Greetings 8

SECOND TEN THINGS NOBODY GIVES A SHIT ABOUT
    Love, or Lust? 9
    Little Shaver 9
    First-Time Mother 10
    Shocked By A Rocker 11
    Unable To Pronounce Or Spell 11
    Strategies 12
    Deathly Silence 13
    The Final Exam 13
    Fancy Bartendering 14
    Free 15

THIRD TEN THINGS NOBODY GIVES A SHIT ABOUT
    Glory Days 17
    Problems 17
    Wedding Reception... 18
    The Son-In-Law 18
    Royal Visitors 19
    The Reunion 20
    Award-Winning Salesman 21
    Weather Report 21
    Fired Up 22
    Baby's Name 22

FOURTH TEN THINGS NOBODY GIVES A SHIT ABOUT
    Hot MaMa 23
    World's Greatest Athlete 23
    Science Fiction 24
    Raising The Roof 24
    Tweetin' and Tootin' 25
    Lethal Force 26
    Vote 26
    Singing Up A Storm 27
    Housecleaning 28
    In Confidence 28

FIFTH TEN THINGS NOBODY GIVES A SHIT ABOUT
    Messing With Halloween 29
    Famous By Association 30
    King Tut Tut Tut 30
    True Love 31
    Worldbeater Son 31
    Time To Tell 32
    Fast Car 32
    The Activist 33
    Genius 34
    Political Flip-Flop 34

SIXTH TEN THINGS NOBODY GIVES A SHIT ABOUT
    Fashion Plates 35
    Engagement's Off 35
    The Crash 36
    When Dey Is Nose To Nose 36
    The Golfer 37
    Money Man 38
    Ink 39
    Scandal 40
    Footloose 40
    Husband in Training 41

SEVENTH TEN THINGS NOBODY GIVES A SHIT ABOUT
    The Weekend 43
    Holey 44
    D-I-V-O-R-C-E 44

Modern-Day Diet 45
Sleeping Beauty 45
Changing Direction 46
Moving On 46
Sleepyhead 47
Errand Boy 47
They Wear Like Iron 48

EIGHTH TEN THINGS NOBODY GIVES A SHIT ABOUT
Happy Anniversary 49
Record-Setting Pace 50
Purity 50
Swoosh 50
Half Brothers 51
Hidden Tattoo 51
It's In! 52
Correct P-R-O-N-O-U-N-C-I-A-T-I-O-N 53
Skimpy 53
Breaking News 53

NINTH TEN THINGS NOBODY GIVES A SHIT ABOUT
The Shout Out 55
It's News 56
Keep Them Hands In The Air 57
Friendly Difference of Opinion 57
The Outer Circle 58
Bird Watch 59
Averages 59
Hung Over 59
Confused? 60
Cultured 60

TENTH TEN THINGS NOBODY GIVES A SHIT ABOUT
Chump Change 61
No Round Ball 61
The Testimony 62
Medical Alert 63
Salt Of The Earth 64
Broke Jock 64
The Songster 65

  He's Perfect 65
  Working Hard For The Money 66
  Fire Engine Red 68

ELEVENTH TEN THINGS NOBODY GIVES A SHIT ABOUT
  Peace 69
  Politically Incorrect 70
  Short Stuff 70
  Weekender 71
  Directional 71
  The Romantic 72
  Fish Story 73
  Bloody Marys 73
  Chicago, Chicago 74
  Shooting The Shit 74
  Who's Counting? 75

TWELFTH TEN THINGS NOBODY GIVES A SHIT ABOUT
  Shape Up 77
  The Author 78
  All Sold Out 78
  Problem Or Solution? 79
  Love Machine 80
  Slip O' The Tongue 80
  It's Chic, Daahling 81
  Expecting 82
  The Babysitter 82
  Convoluted Justice 83

THIRTEENTH TEN THINGS NOBODY GIVES A SHIT ABOUT
  Rocket Shopper 85
  Child Genius 85
  Red And Green Ones 86
  Rights 87
  Chug-A-Lug 87
  The Boss's Wife 88
  Pie, Anyone? 88
  Involved 89
  Mister Fixerup 90
  Pastry, Anyone? 91

FOURTEENTH TEN THINGS NOBODY GIVES A SHIT ABOUT
    Kindly Professor Wankel 93
    Your Opinion, Please 94
    Bowl Bound 95
    No Longer Seeing Red 95
    Workin' Like A Dog 96
    Who Popped The Country? 97
    Watch This 97
    Above The Grass 98
    Say What? 98
    Break A Leg 99

FIFTEENTH TEN THINGS NOBODY GIVES A SHIT ABOUT
    Who's Who 101
    Oompah 102
    Monkeying Around 102
    No Action 102
    Who You? 103
    No Nibbling 103
    Happiness 104
    Etymology 105
    Telling It Like It Is 106

TO OBTAIN MORE BOOKS 107

YOUR TURN 109

TELLING IT LIKE IT IS . . .

There are a lot of things that nobody gives a shit about. To be honest, nobody cares to hear about your fabulous grandkids, your kidney stones, the touchdown you almost scored thirty years ago, or the worthless bastard who's married to your daughter.

Now, in case you're not aware of what else nobody gives a shit about, here are over one hundred forty real-life situations that might give you a clue. And, if you choose to ignore this sound advice, don't be surprised if somebody looks you square in the eye and says, "Who Gives A Shit."

FIRST
TEN THINGS NOBODY GIVES A SHIT ABOUT

REJECTION

We sent this manuscript to a high-powered literary agent from New York City who replied with a form rejection letter and a handwritten note saying, "This does not qualify as *LITERATURE!!*"

We wrote back and said,

"Who Gives A Shit."

BUBBA DAY

The announcer on the radio says that June 2 is *National Bubba Day*, which honors anybody named Bubba. Our first reaction is, "You've gotta be shittin' me." Our second reaction is,

"Who Gives A Shit."

DOORBUSTER

    It is an age-old shopping philosophy passed down from mothers to daughters since the beginning of time – If something is on sale at a deep, deep discount, buy it, even if you don't need it or have no use for it. And, if your husband cannot understand this simple logic,

Who Gives A Shit.

BLACKLISTED

    Brittni is horribly upset that she and her husband, Albert, did not get invited to the Clayton/Willaby wedding. Albert, who can be quite philosophical, sometimes, says "There'll be other weddings, so . . .

Who Gives A Shit."

HUH?

When the Boss conducts a meeting of the employees, he likes to use acronyms instead of stating things in full to save time and also probably to show off. He assumes that all employees are up to speed on all of the acronyms and understand what they mean, which might be an erroneous assumption on his part. He's about to begin the meeting – let's listen in.

"If we can raise the GDR above the LPTL and keep the MCV at its current level while we maximize the ORSD and minimize the IBFH, we should have a good chance to reach our YAG for the NFY. Any questions?"

Smedley, sitting in the back row says, "Have you considered WGAS?"

"WGAS . . ." the Boss says. "I'm, I'm not familiar with that term."

Smedley, who is no longer employed at the company at the time of this writing, replies . . .

"Who Gives A Shit."

Peter Davidson

LONG LIVER

Mark is a fitness fanatic and health food nut who works out three hours a day and eats only wheat germ, soy burgers, alfalfa sprouts, rice cakes, and dried ginger roots and drinks only sterilized goat milk and coconut water. He brags that he will probably live to be a hundred and ten years old.

The guys down at Ruebin's Pub, drinking beer and eating pretzels, say if that's what it takes to live to be a hundred and ten ...

Who Gives A Shit.

BREAKING NEWS

The tabloids report that alleged actress Brigette Mimeaux just broke up with her boyfriend.

Who Gives A Shit.

HOW YA DOIN'?

Sam was in the grocery store, slowly wheeling his shopping cart down the breakfast cereal aisle, when he met a guy, Herman, that he knew casually. Slightly, actually.

"How ya doin'?" Sam says, trying to be kind, as he wheeled on past Herman. Of course, Sam expected Herman to reply, "Good, how ya doin'?" as he continued on his way. No such luck.

Herman stops in his tracks and looks at Sam with sad, drooping eyes. "Not so good," he says. Immediately Sam wished he'd have kept his damn mouth shut.

Then, Herman goes on to explain, in excruciating detail, the dozen or so health calamities that he is battling including gout, erectile dysfunction, swollen gonads, ringing ears, blurred vision, water on the knee, restless leg syndrome, lumbago, and bowel obstruction.

Not to sound unsympathetic, Herman, but . . .

Who Gives A Shit.

SOCIALITE BOOK

Socialite Yvette is famous for being famous – or for having a rich grandfather, or for having a boyfriend who secretly taped one of their sexual encounters which was subsequently sold to some porn company and distributed around the globe. Socialite Yvette is now writing her autobiography and promises to divulge various startling secrets. Hey, Miss Socialite,

Who Gives A Shit.

HOLIDAY GREEETINGS

It's one of the happiest times of the year, when people exchange greeting cards with people that they haven't thought of since last year's holiday season and who they haven't seen for twenty or thirty years and who they hope they don't see again for another twenty years.

Often accompanying that greeting card is "The Letter," which is a photocopied mini family biography detailing the fabulous careers of their children and the record-setting exploits of their snot-nosed grandkids, none of whom you've ever met and never want to meet. To be honest, it's nice to be remembered once a year with a greeting card, but as for "The Letter,"

Who Gives A Shit.

SECOND
TEN THINGS NOBODY GIVES A SHIT ABOUT

LOVE, OR LUST?

The news is spreading through the family like a wildfire – eighty-nine-year-old grandma is moving in with her ninety-year-old boyfriend and everybody has an opinion. Here's one –

Who Gives A Shit.

LITTLE SHAVER

A guy at work, Roger, brags that his thirteen-year-old son is so mature that he shaves every morning. Roger, if your thirteen-year-old son was able to buy beer, that would be something to brag about – but shaving . . .

Who Gives A Shit.

FIRST-TIME MOTHER

Cynthia is a first-time mother at age 36. She is so enthralled with being a mother that she plans to write a book on the "Trials and Difficulties of Motherhood." Beverly, who gave birth to five children and raised them to adulthood says, "When it comes to your opinions about motherhood,

Who Gives A Shit."

SHOCKED BY A ROCKER

Suzie is so proud to be the girlfriend of Willie, the drummer of the Rock 'N' Roll band, *Daddy's Money*. But, that only lasted until she showed up unexpectedly to surprise Willie at the band's concert in San Francisco, where she discovered that he also has another girlfriend on the side.

Suzie, honey, he's a musician! If you want to continue to be Willie's girlfriend, when it comes to other women, you've got to develop an attitude of . . .

Who Gives A Shit.

UNABLE TO PRONOUNCE OR SPELL

All her life, Mary Jones felt that she was hindered by having such a common and ordinary name, so when her daughter was born she was determined to do better for her by giving her a unique name – Jil-ean. Of course, nobody can read it when they see it and nobody can spell it when they hear it but you've got to admit, it's not common or ordinary.

In case you haven't figured it out – the dash isn't silent, so it's pronounced "Jildashean." Of course you think it's goofy but Mary and Jil-ean like it, and if they like it . . .

Who Gives A Shit.

STRATEGIES

If a company's original plan or strategy fails to work out as anticipated, the tendency is to go to "Plan B," which, loosely translated, means "We have no idea what the hell's going on, but let's fake it." If "Plan B" fails, the tendency is to go to "Plan C," which is to find a scapegoat to blame it on and, even though it isn't fair, we're in the clear so . . .

Who Gives A Shit.

DEATHLY SILENCE

Warren is a single man who has resorted to using a dating service to try to find a girlfriend. He has carefully studied the profiles of numerous women on the site and has sent his personal information to at least a dozen women. He is irritated that none of them has had the decency and courtesy to even respond to his messages, even if it is to tell him they're not interested. I hate to break the news to you, Warren, but silence *is* a message – and it means . . .

Who Gives A Shit.

THE FINAL EXAM

Bill missed the final exam for his college Accounting course because his dog ate his alarm clock and also ate his car keys. Professor Horner has news for Bill.

Who Gives A Shit.

FANCY BARTENDERING

The bartenders at *Celestial,* a high class night club, must have all attended the same bartender school where they learned to do juggling tricks with the bottles before them pour or serve them. For example, before they serve a bottle of beer, they spin it on their finger, throw it in the air and catch it behind their back, walk the length of the bar balancing the bottle on their nose, and then open the bottle with their teeth. By the time they get around to serving it, the beer is warm, the bottle is ready to explode, and the customer is dying of thirst, so when it comes to the juggling and bottle tricks . . .

Who Gives A Shit.

FREE

It took John a long while to figure out that he no longer can afford all the free stuff being offered to him. For instance, those free cocktails at that Las Vegas casino ended up costing him about $65 each. That free bottle of weight loss pills cost John $150 for the bottles of pills they automatically sent him the following month and that free telephone service tied him in knots for five years. That is why these days when someone offers him something and says, "But, it's free," John cordially replies,

"Who Gives A Shit."

THIRD
TEN THINGS NOBODY GIVES A SHIT ABOUT

GLORY DAYS

Charlie is forty-eight years old, which means that he graduated from high school about thirty years ago. Every chance he gets, especially when he's had a few beers, he likes to relive the football conference championship game. If Anderson hadn't missed his block and if the coach hadn't put the wrong guy in at right guard and if the quarterback hadn't thrown the ball so hard, and if the field hadn't been so wet and soggy and the grass hadn't been so long, Charlie would have caught the pass that would have won the game and thus the championship.

Who Gives A Shit.

PROBLEMS

So, you got problems, Bubba, you got problems. I hate to tell you this, but 25% of the people you know are glad that you got 'em and of the other 75% of the people you know, there's nobody . . .

Who Gives A Shit.

WEDDING RECEPTION

The bride-to-be has been fretting over the wedding reception details for months. Among other things, she can't decide if sandwiches should be served on buns or on bread and if there should be mixed nuts or just plain peanuts.

Sweetie, as long as the beer is cold,

Who Gives A Shit.

THE SON-IN-LAW

The guy sitting at the end of the bar seems like a nice enough guy – until someone asks him about his family. He has one child – a daughter who is thirty-two years old, and who is beautiful, intelligent, and talented. And then he describes the low-down, miserable, lazy, rotten, worthless, free-loading son-of-a-bitch that she's married to. Thanks for sharing, but

Who Gives A Shit.

ROYAL VISITORS

Every newspaper, magazine, radio station and television station is going nuts over the upcoming visit by the King and Queen of some country that normal people can't pronounce and couldn't locate on a map. The King and Queen coming to America . . .

Who Gives A Shit.

THE REUNION

It's the fifteen year class reunion and somebody got the brilliant idea that everyone should stand up and tell about their life since high school graduation, using a microphone so everyone can hear them loud and clear, nonetheless.

Bob was great. He said, "I'm Bob and I've been a mechanic for the past fifteen years." Wonderful speech.

Albert just got out of prison and is happy to see everyone. "But, "I'm innocent," he said. Whose bright idea was it to invite Albert? At least his speech was short and to the point. And, it was captivating.

Martha has five kids ages 17, 13, 11, 9, and 7. The seventeen-year-old daughter is both beautiful and brilliant. The thirteen-year-old is a musical prodigy and can play five different instruments, all at the same time. The eleven-year-old was voted by his classmates as the most handsome, most comical, most caring, most . . ."

Who Gives A Shit.

AWARD-WINNING SALESMAN

An article in the local newspaper says that life insurance salesman Lenny Boggess attended his company's annual convention and received the Golden Circle Award for outstanding life insurance sales.

Who Gives A Shit.

WEATHER REPORT

The television weather man reports that the temperature in Death Valley, California reached 125 degrees today.

Who Gives A Shit.

FIRED UP

A raging midnight fire completely destroyed the business that Roland had built from the ground up over a twenty-year period. Roland's friend, Nancy, tried to console him, saying how terribly sorry she was that Roland's lifetime work had been destroyed. Roland replied, "A good fire is worth two bankruptcies, so . . .

Who Gives A Shit."

BABY'S NAME

A supermodel and her athlete husband just had a child and made a public announcement that the child's name is Chastity.

Who Gives A Shit.

FOURTH
TEN THINGSNOBODY GIVES A SHIT ABOUT

HOT MAMA

    Rumor has it that a local woman was seduced by the entire offensive line of the football team, the trombone section of the marching band, and a guy named Weasel Hammermeister. As long as it isn't your mother, sister, wife, or daughter . . .

Who Gives A Shit.

WORLD'S GREATEST ATHLETE

    Max says he is the world's greatest athlete, aged 60. He can ride his bike 25 miles a day, swim for two hours without stopping, bench press 300 pounds, out-ski the teenagers, and still drink a half gallon of Tequila every night. Max . . .

Who Gives A Shit.

SCIENCE FICTION

Scientists recently rechecked their math and discovered that the North Star is actually thirty percent closer to earth than previously believed – only 323 light-years away.

Who Gives A Shit.

RAISING THE ROOF

Franklin Bank, which pays interest of .0125% on its savings accounts (As in 13 cents per year on a $1,000 investment), has just announced that it is increasing its interest rate by fifty percent.

Who Gives A Shit.

TWEETIN' AND TOOTIN'

Sara asked her uncle, John, if he tweets. He said, "No, but I toot a lot." She wasn't amused.

Sara signed John up as one of her followers and she insisted that he check in on her from time to time. So, today he did. There were over a hundred tweets and this is what he learned.

This morning Sara woke up before the alarm went off. She had toast, slightly burnt, with strawberry jam, orange juice, and coffee for breakfast. She took out the garbage before leaving for work.

Sara had a hard time finding a parking spot in the shade when she arrived at work and had to settle for a parking spot without shade.

Sara got to work a few minutes early, so she went to the restroom before going to her desk.

Sara stubbed her toe on the curb when she returned from lunch but it didn't hurt at all. Her office chair squeaks when she swivels. Sara went to the restroom twice this afternoon. After work, Sara . . . .

Sara, honey,

Who Gives A Shit.

LETHAL FORCE

William says that last night he broke wind and passed gas with such force, volume, and density that he set off the carbon monoxide detector. Besides his wife,

Who Gives A Shit.

VOTE

Perkins and Williams, two idiots, are running for mayor of the town of Mergen and they both want everyone's vote. The local newspaper is interviewing residents to see who they think would be the best mayor. Snodgrass said it best . . .

"Who Gives A Shit."

SINGING UP A STORM

It's Karaoke night at the Regency Lounge and Charlie is on stage delivering a rousing version of "Proud Mary." Sure, Charlie lost the melody halfway through the first verse, hit a couple of notes they don't even have on the charts yet, and screeched one glass-shattering note that caused every dog within six blocks to howl, but the beer is cold and Charlie's with friends, so . . .

Who Gives A Shit.

HOUSECLEANING

Candice is so embarrassed. Four of her husband's friends showed up unexpectedly, so she didn't have a chance to dust and vacuum the house before they arrived. Candice, these are guys, so . . .

Who Gives A Shit.

IN CONFIDENCE

I feel honored that you chose me to confide in about your personal, financial, marital, and sexual problems. Unfortunately, you have confused me with someone . . .

Who Gives A Shit.

FIFTH
TEN THINGS NOBODY GIVES A SHIT ABOUT

MESSING WITH HALLOWEEN

For some reason, Curtis is obsessed with Count Dracula and has become convinced that instead of being a brutal blood-sucking murderous son-of-a-bitch, as he is normally portrayed in movies and at Halloween time, Dracula was actually a good guy who was misunderstood. Curtis is researching Dracula's background in Albania, Transylvania, Hungary, Poland, and Wallachia, among other countries. Curtis believes that he will be able to prove that Count Dracula was actually a kind, gentle, and misunderstood good guy.

Who Gives A Shit.

FAMOUS BY ASSOCIATION

So, Sam says his second cousin's wife was a cousin to the 1980's Rock 'N' Roller Sam "Space Cadet" Cadeo, who had a top 50 record on the charts.

Who Gives A Shit.

KING TUT TUT TUT

Archeologists have just uncovered a tomb that they believe was the final resting place of King Tut Tut Tut and they are convinced, after examining The King's remains, that he may have been only four feet eight inches tall.

Who Gives A Shit.

TRUE LOVE

An eighty-three year old billionaire just announced that he is engaged to a twenty-five year old former Playmate-of-the-Year.

Who Gives A Shit.

WORLDBEATER SON

Ben says his son graduated at the top of his class at Harvard, passed the Bar Exam on his first try, became a partner in a big law firm, then moved on to become lead legal counsel at a major corporation where he makes millions of dollars a year, and he owns houses in Florida, Arizona, Hawaii, France, Spain, Greece, New Zealand and South Africa.

Who Gives A Shit.

TIME TO TELL

A seventy-two-year-old woman is making the talk show programs hawking her recently published book in which she claims that when she was a teenager she was deflowered by a boy who, many years later, became President of the United States.

Who Gives A Shit.

FAST CAR

Herman bought a new foreign car and proudly reports that he took it out on the highway and wound up to 155 miles an hour.

Who Gives A Shit.

THE ACTIVIST

It seems that when someone becomes famous as an actor, actress, or musician, they believe that it behooves them to become an activist for some cause. Some adopt causes for homeless children or abandoned pets. Others help fight dread diseases or try to free innocent people from jail. Still others work for political reform or the safety of children's toys.

When Bonnie, "Boom Boom," Bates became famous on a beach bum television show for wearing skimpy bikinis and uttering memorable dialog like, "The sun is hot today," and "Ooh, that lifeguard is sooo hot," she decided she, too, should become an activist. She searched desperately for a cause to champion, but all the good stuff seemed to be taken. Then one night while eating chicken cordon bleu, it hit her right between the eyes – she would become an activist against cruelty to chickens.

Well, Boom Boom, that's a lovely thought, but as anyone who ever grew up on a chicken farm will tell you, live chickens are disgusting, uncontrollable, ornery, ugly, squawking scourges of the earth. So, sorry to tell you this, Miss Activist, but you should pick a different cause because when it comes to cruelty to chickens, there's nobody . . .

Who Gives A Shit.

GENIUS

Marcus smugly informs the group that he is a member of MENSA, the international high IQ society.

Who Gives A Shit.

POLITICAL FLIP-FLOP

Alleged actor, Alexander Hamilton, has announced that he is switching his loyalty from the Republican party to the Libertarian party.

Who Gives A Shit.

SIXTH
TEN THINGS NOBODY GIVES A SHIT ABOUT

FASHION PLATES

    The fashion designers of the world have decided that it's time men stop wearing the same old styles and become more fashionable. Thus, they have redesigned every piece of men's apparel. Pants will be shiny and will fit snuggly, suit coats will hang down to the knees, and shirts will have bright circles, squares, and triangles. Hey, designers, when it comes to adopting the newest fad in clothing, do you really think there's any guy out there . . .

Who Gives A Shit.

ENGAGEMENT'S OFF

    A twenty-five year old former Playmate-of-the-Year announced that she has broken off her engagement to her eighty-three year old billionaire finance.

Who Gives A Shit.

THE CRASH

The stock market crashed today, dropping over thirty percent in the afternoon alone. To us guys working the night shift at McDonalds hamburger shop,

Who Gives A Shit.

WHEN DEY IS NOSE TO NOSE

Melissa, who is 6' 2" is dating Jonathan, who is 5' 3" and to kiss her, Jonathan has to stand on a five-gallon pail. And then there's that indisputable law of physics: "When dey is nose to nose his toes . . . and when dey is toes to toes his nose . . ."

Well, they seem to like it, so . . .

Who Gives A Shit.

THE GOLFER

Randy just finished eighteen holes of golf, grabbed himself a cocktail, and joined a group of guys who also just finished their round.

"How did it go?" some idiot asks.

"I hit my drive off the first tee 240 yards straight as a frozen rope, using my two wood. Next I hit my three iron about 200 yards to the apron of the green. I hit the ball within two feet of the pin with my pitching wedge and one-putted for a birdie.

"I used my seven iron for my tee shot on the 180-yard second hole and shanked a high looper to the right and hit a tree and then, as luck would have it, the ball bounced right into the middle of the fairway, thirty yards from the green. I used my nine iron and hit it a little too hard but . . ." Randy, Randy –

Who Gives A Shit.

MONEY MAN

Joe is a mechanic who earned $45,000 from his employer last year, yet he deposited $75,000 into his checking account, which drew the attention of the Internal Revenue Service. Joe was called in for an income tax audit and was asked to explain the discrepancy. Joe explained that he had regularly put a dollar bill into a coffee can each and every week for quite some time. When the total reached $30,000, he had simply deposited the dollar bills in his checking account. Simple.

Joe's letter from the IRS explained that by saving a dollar a week it would have taken Joe 576 years and 48 weeks to accumulate the $30,000.

Thus, Joe's explanation was disallowed and Joe owed an additional $16,340 in unpaid income taxes, penalties, and interest. When it comes to listening to taxpayers' explanations, apparently the Internal Revenue Service is not someone . . .

Who Gives A Shit.

INK

The story is in every tabloid, newspaper, and magazine, and is all over the internet – thirteen-year-old singing sensation Collin David just got his first tattoo but he won't reveal (1) The tattoo's image, and (2) Where it is placed.

(1) Who Gives A Shit. (2) Who Gives A Shit.

SCANDAL

Hoping to jumpstart his fledging acting career by creating some notoriety, Johnny Miller leaked to the internet a video of him and his girlfriend having sex. The bold move had an immediate impact on his career, plunging it into the depths of obscurity. Apparently, Johnny Miller can't act, and when it came to watching his sexual prowess, it also appears that there's nobody out there . . .

Who Gives A Shit.

FOOTLOOSE

Janine owns over 150 pair of shoes, which drives her husband, Art, wild. He can't see why anyone would buy a pair of shoes and wear them only once, or never at all, or why Janine keeps buying shoes since she already has so many. Janine's response is simple, "Art, honey, when it comes to your opinion about me and my shoes . . .

Who Gives A Shit."

HUSBAND IN TRAINING

Jack was having a fantastic year selling used cars so he decided to give his wife, Diane, something special, and very expensive, for their first wedding anniversary. Jack led Diane into the living room where he had placed a huge box that he had wrapped personally.

With great anticipation and a big smile on her face, Diane slowly unwrapped the box – and came face to face with a magnificent vacuum cleaner. It was obvious that Diane was overwhelmed by Jack's generosity as she broke down crying. Jack, ever the salesman, felt the need to seal the deal and said, "That's the finest machine that money can buy."

As any man who has been married for over two years could have predicted, Diane wiped away her tears, gave Jack a look that could kill, and said,

"Who Gives A Shit."

SEVENTH
TEN THINGS NOBODY GIVES A SHIT ABOUT

THE WEEKEND

"How was your weekend?" Someone offhandedly asked Mel on Monday morning as he came into work.

"Well," Mel replied, "on Saturday morning I got up at the crack of dawn, ate a quick breakfast, straightened out the stuff in the garage and mowed the lawn, all before 9 a.m. Then I fixed the leaking downspout, washed and waxed the car, replaced the broken window in the storage shed, and put up a basketball hoop for the kids. Then, I went to the store and bought some wood, screws, nails, and paint to build a . . ."

Mel, oh Mel – the short version would have been fine, but as to the long version,

Who Gives A Shit.

HOLEY

A recent survey of 1,000 American men found that over 90% of them often wear underwear with holes in them and that their wives are absolutely appalled. The survey further found that when it comes to their wife's opinion on the topic, there's only 5% of the 90% . . .

Who Gives A Shit.

D-I-V-O-R-C-E

Two B-list movie stars, Michelle and Michael, announced that they are getting a divorce but will remain best friends.

Who Gives A Shit.

MODERN-DAY DIET

Some crazed health nut wrote a diet book and claims that if a man gave up drinking beer for a month he would lose up to ten pounds.

Who Gives A Shit.

SLEEPING BEAUTY

Rumor has it that 80-year-old grandpa sleeps in the nude. Other than the fact that it might take ten years off someone's life if they wandered into his bedroom by accident at an inopportune time . . .

Who Gives A Shit.

CHANGING DIRECTION

Stay with me on this. Charlene was born a girl but really felt more like she was a boy so when she was thirty years old she had an operation to remove a few body parts and add a few others and now she - er, he – is known as Charles. Charles has written a book describing the transformation.

Who Gives A Shit.

MOVING ON

The city council proposed to widen the street past Jerome's house from two lanes to four lanes. This upset Jerome horribly and he drafted petitions and organized marches and council meeting sit-ins to protest the council's proposal. Finally, the council took their final vote and, against all of Jerome's protests, they decided to go ahead with widening the street. As a final protest, Jerome is threatening to move out of town. Jerome,

Who Gives A Shit.

SLEEPYHEAD

Hoping to curry some sympathy from the boss, Ed explains that he was restless last night and only got three hours of sleep. The boss's response was predictable –

Who Gives A Shit.

ERRAND BOY

Sam's wife sent him to the store to buy three cans of *House-and-Home* brand lilac-scented air fresheners. He returned with four cans of *Farm-and-Home* brand rose-scented air fresheners, which upset his wife to the point of tears.

Sam thinks she's overreacting because when it comes to air fresheners,

Who Gives A Shit.

THEY WEAR LIKE IRON

After deep contemplation, James determined that what wears out a pair of pants isn't wearing 'em, its *washing 'em*. Therefore, in an effort to get as much use out of his pants as possible, James wears a pair of pants for a week at a time without washing them, maybe two. And, if this frugal strategy offends thee,

Who Gives A Shit.

EIGHTH
TEN THINGS NOBODY GIVES A SHIT ABOUT

HAPPY ANNIVERSARY

    Harry and Anne had been married for nine years and Harry had become increasingly unhappy being married. He longed to be single again and wanted a divorce. However, Harry did not want to be known among their friends and relatives as the guy who had deserted his wife Anne. So, Harry devised a plan that would lead to Anne's being so disgusted with him that she would throw him out. As an added touch, just to make sure that the plan worked, Harry decided to drop the news on her on their wedding anniversary.

    "Anne," Harry said, "I have something to tell you. I have had an affair and I don't blame you for . . .

    Anne interrupted Harry before he could finish . . .

"Who Gives A Shit."

RECORD-SETTING PACE

The *Sidewinders* semi-professional rugby team just lost its twelfth game in a row. Other than the miserable bastard who owns the team,

Who Gives A Shit.

PURITY

Dennis, a confirmed bachelor, proudly announced on his thirty-fifth birthday that he is still a virgin.

Who Gives A Shit.

SWOOSH

Gary proudly boasts that he has purchased a new electronic remote control gadget that allows him to flush the toilet from up to sixty feet away.

Who Gives A Shit.

HALF BROTHERS

Bill claims that The Traveling Wilburys was a band consisting of five members who all had the same mother but different fathers. Roger argues that the band members all had the same father but different mothers. Either way, the band was damn good, so . . .

Who Gives A Shit.

HIDDEN TATTOO

Harold just got his girlfriend's name tattooed on his butt. Other than the fact that this lovelorn decision will someday come back to bite him in the ass,

Who Gives A Shit.

IT'S IN!

Let's stand together on a busy city sidewalk for an hour and observe women on their way to work. Amazing, isn't it!

Let us critique their fashion sense. Almost everyone has the same style of shoes and their skirts, dresses, blouses, and coats likewise are almost identical to each other's in style, color, patterns, and fit.

So, how did this happen that almost everyone is dressed similarly to each other? It's simple – they're wearing what they're wearing because *It's In*. Some clothing designer somewhere, or maybe it's a conspiracy of clothing designers, decided that this year *This*, whatever that is, is going to be *In*, and so it is.

Next year, if the clothing designers go berserk and decide that women should wear shoes with thick soles and squatty square heels, dresses that go down to their ankles, and disposable blouses made from old newspapers will women wear them? Of course they will, because *It's In* – and beyond that . . .

Who Gives A Shit.

CORRECT P-R-O-N-O-U-N-C-I-A-T-I-O-N

The English teacher demands that when pronouncing a word that starts with the letters "WH," as in "White," the "H" be pronounced first as in "HuhWite." Hey, Teach – this class is full of a bunch of us numbnuts who can barely read and can't spell - therefore, when it comes to fancy words, there's nobody . . .

Who Gives A Shit.

SKIMPY

Bob's wife is aghast at the short skirt that barely covers the butt of that cute blonde over there and that shows damn near everything when she bends over. Bob, being more open-minded, replies . . .

"Who Gives A Shit."

BREAKING NEWS

The tabloids report that former child star and alleged actress, Emma Hayes, has been jailed.

Who Gives A Shit.

NINTH
TEN THINGS NOBODY GIVES A SHIT ABOUT

THE SHOUT OUT

Three days before Gaylord Ownazorgy was to graduate from high school, he was seated next to his girlfriend in the packed auditorium, listening to the spring concert by the high school band. The band was playing louder and louder and the director was whipping the band into a frenzy. Gaylord said something to his girlfriend but the band was too loud for her to hear. He yelled his message to her but still she could not hear. He reared back, filled his lungs with air, and yelled to her as loud as he could, "I'd like to . . ."

At that precise moment, the director cut off the band and Gaylord finished his sentence, yelling at the top of his lungs, in a totally silent auditorium . . . "Fuck You."

That moment, which is still known throughout the county as "The Ownazorgy," happened twenty-five years ago. In fact, throughout the county, *The Ownazorgy* is used to measure time, as in BTO (Before The Ownazorgy) or ATO (After The Ownazorgy).

Gaylord Ownazorgy left town a week after the incident and never returned.

The local newspaper is writing an article to commemorate the twenty-fifth anniversary of "The Ownazorgy" and contacted Gaylord asking for a quote.

All Gaylord would say was, "That was twenty-five years ago and it didn't happen. But if it did happen, it was somebody else, not me. And what they said wasn't what everybody thinks it was; it was 'Lucky you.' Beyond that, and you can quote me on this . . .

Who Gives A Shit."

IT'S NEWS

The *National Tattletale* tabloid is making a big deal out of the fact that they caught television evening news anchor Ted Miller wearing the same necktie on the air twice in one week. Obviously, *Tattletaler*, it was a slow news week for you because when it comes to what necktie Ted Miller wears, there is nobody out here in TV land . . .

Who Gives A Shit.

KEEP THEM HANDS IN THE AIR
　　The Jesse James Gang committed the first train robbery in the world on July 21, 1874, in Adair, Iowa. Most likely, there isn't even anyone in Adair, Iowa . . .

　　Who Gives A Shit.

FRIENDLY DIFFERENCE OF OPINION
　　My friend, it is so rare these days to find someone like you who is intelligent, knowledgeable, and informed who is willing to listen to and consider my viewpoints on politics, even though they are not the same as yours. And, now, after intently listening to my viewpoints, you want to share yours with me. Actually, when it comes to your political viewpoints, I'm not someone . . .

　　Who Gives A Shit.

THE OUTER CIRCLE

At the company where Joe works, management brings in motivational speakers two or three times a year to conduct training sessions for the employees. Today, Dr. Spunderman from a thousand miles away, with degrees in both psychology and philosophy, is conducting the program.

Prior to today's meeting, Dr. Spunderman arranged all of the chairs in circles with five chairs in an inner circle and ten chairs in an outer circle around the outside of the five chairs in the inner circle.

Everyone was given a packet of information when they entered the room and the packet had either a red or a green circle on the back of the folder. Anyone with a red circle was to sit on a chair in the inner circle. Anyone with a green circle was to sit on a chair on the outer circle. Everyone is now seated on their chairs.

Dr. Spunderman asks the people sitting in the inner circle how they feel. Their responses include "Privileged," "Special," "Superior," and "Powerful."

Next, Dr. Spunderman asks the people sitting in the outer circle how they feel. Their responses include, "Inferior," "Neglected," "Second-rate," "and "Unworthy."

Joe, sitting in the outer circle, and who is no longer an employee of the company at the time of this writing, replies, "This is just a game, so . . .

Who Gives A Shit."

BIRD WATCH

An article in the newspaper says that seven members of the local Bird Club went on a field trip to the woods south of town and counted eight Red Breasted Blackbirds in a two-hour observation period.

Who Gives A Shit.

AVERAGES

When Myles moved from the state of New York to the state of New Jersey, the average I.Q. of both states went up. Except for the residents of New Jersey,

Who Gives A Shit.

HUNG OVER

Bill says that he drank too much last night and has a ferocious hangover.

Who Gives A Shit.

CONFUSED?

Charley's wife tells everybody that Charley can't keep his days straight – he thinks Monday is Tuesday, Thursday is Wednesday, and sometimes that Tuesday is Thursday. Charley's response is that he's retired and every day's a Saturday, so . . .

Who Gives A Shit.

CULTURED

Much to the chagrin of his high-society mother-in-law, John is a cultural barbarian who doesn't know the difference between Beethoven's Fifth Movement and a bowel movement and furthermore, his general attitude seems to be . . .

Who Gives A Shit.

TENTH
TEN THINGS NOBODY GIVES A SHIT ABOUT

CHUMP CHANGE

The financial press says that billionaire Waldo McCracken lost fifty million dollars in the stock market last week.

Who Gives A Shit.

NO ROUND BALL

The greedy millionaire professional basketball players and the greedy billionaire owners of the professional basketball teams are fighting over how to divide up billions of dollars in revenue and are threatening to cancel this year's season. None of them have even uttered the word, "Fans," during their negotiations.

Perhaps they're not aware, but when it comes to canceling the season, there's more to do in this town than go to a basketball game, so . . .

Who Gives A Shit.

THE TESTIMONY

Robert belongs to a religious group where people regularly stand up during the service and give a testimony about how they had been dragged down to the depths of hell by the devil, but then how they rose up and overcame their problem and defeated the devil. For instance, Alice was a successful Author who was married to a former professional baseball player who started a string of successful fitness centers. They had a wonderful life until the devil interfered and convinced Alice's husband to run off with his voluptuous twenty-three year-old assistant, which ruined Alice's life and thrust her into the depths of despair. Finally, Alice confronted the devil and exposed his dirty deeds in a new book that became a bestseller.

Robert felt terrible because his life was wonderful and he had no testimony to share at a service. But then, Robert got fired from his job for no reason at all – the work of the devil - and he eventually ended up homeless, living off of handouts.

Robert decided to fight back and he engaged the devil in hand-to-hand combat under a highway bridge and defeated the devil. During the battle, he noticed a crack in the bridge and he informed the highway department, who rewarded Robert with a high paying job as a bridge inspector.

Even though Robert is suspected of making it up, it's a damn good story and he got his testimony, so ...

Who Gives A Shit.

MEDICAL ALERT

A breaking news story reports that the entire Kardashian clan has come down with laryngitis and their television program, "Keeping Up With The Kardashians," will be cancelled for at least two weeks.

Who Gives A Shit.

SALT OF THE EARTH

The waiter at the restaurant, eager to display his knowledge of the culinary arts, makes a big deal out of the fact that their salt shakers contain sea salt rather than iodized salt. Hey buddy,

Who Gives A Shit.

BROKE JOCK

Marvin was a professional football player who played in two Super Bowls, was an all-pro six times, and earned a total of seventy-five million dollars in his fourteen year career. Marvin retired two years ago, at age thirty-six, and filed for bankruptcy yesterday. You blew it, Bubba, and that's why there's nobody . . .

Who Gives A Shit.

THE SONGSTER

Bill says the song was recorded by Styx. Wally insists that it was Aerosmith. Styx; I know it. Aerosmith, dammit. Styx - Aerosmith. Styx – Aerosmith. Styx – Aerosmith. Aerosmith - Styx.

Who Gives A Shit.

HE'S PERFECT

Debbie readily admits to herself that her fiancé, Harold, can't dance, can't sing, can't carry on much of a conversation, doesn't have a sense of humor, is arrogant, and is a little weird, but since he also has ten million dollar$$$ . . .

Who Gives A Shit.

WORKING HARD FOR THE MONEY

Herman is getting on in years and decides it is time to write his Last Will and Testament. Since he has been a bachelor all his life and has no children, he decides to leave his considerable fortune to his eight nephews and nieces, all of whom have been kind to him, perhaps anticipating that this day would eventually occur.

Herman is a renowned jokester, known for pulling pranks on just about anyone who wasn't on their toes.

Herman wrote his will in his own words and then took it to his long-time lawyer, Leo, for him to review. As Leo reads The Will he smiles, snorts, chortles, laughs, and frowns. You see, Herman was going to have one last laugh at the expense of his nephews and nieces and he wrote his will in code.

For instance, one passage says, "The combination to the large safe in the basement is as follows:

(1) Turn the dial clockwise until you reach a number that is calculated by subtracting the sum of the first two digits of my birth year from the last two digits of the year that I entered the army.

(2) Turn the dial counterclockwise and go past a number twice, stopping at the number the third time. The number is calculated by adding the sum of the digits of the day of my birthday and

adding to it the sum of the last two digits of the year in which I was born.

(3) Turn the dial clockwise and go past a number once, stopping at the number the second time. The number is calculated by adding the last two numbers of my social security number and subtracting the first digit of my social security number from that total.

(4) Turn the dial counterclockwise and go past a number twice, stopping at the number the third time. The number is calculated by taking the number of my mother's birthday day and subtracting it from the number of my father's birthday day.

(5) Open the safe.

And, that's just the first of dozens of similar items in The Will.

"Herman," Leo says, "it will take your nephews and nieces months, if not years, to figure all of this stuff out."

Herman says,

"Who Gives A Shit."

FIRE ENGINE RED

The news media is making a big deal out of the fact that Bjorn Anderson is the first red-headed tennis player to ever win the U. S. Open.

Who Gives A Shit.

ELEVENTH
TEN THINGS NOBODY GIVES A SHIT ABOUT

PEACE

    Martha and Harvey have been married for over sixty-two years and now that they are apparently nearing the end of their lives, they each secretly have the same goal – to outlive the other by just one day so they can have one day of peace and quiet before they die.

    Harvey was just diagnosed with Stage Five cancer and the prognosis is that Harvey won't live for more than a couple of days. Martha's official public comment to friends and relatives is, "We've had a great life together and I'm so sad that Harvey won't be with me very much longer."

    Her private, unspoken, thoughts are . . .

"Who Gives A Shit."

POLITICALLY INCORRECT

Smitty knows that when Margaret bragged about her six-year-old grandson hitting three home runs in a peewee baseball game it would have been politically correct to respond by saying something like, "Wow, that's great – he might be a major leaguer some day." That's why Margaret was thoroughly pissed off when Smitty said,

"Who Gives A Shit."

SHORT STUFF

Sure it's short, but by the time they find that out it's too late to do anything about it anyway, so . . .

Who Gives A Shit.

WEEKENDER

Michelle shows up for work on Monday morning and explains that her painful sunburned face is the result of a faaabbulous weekend ski trip to Aspen.

Who Gives A Shit.

DIRECTIONAL

Dave and his wife, Bev, are visiting with their friends, Bob and Barb, when the conversation turns to traveling. Bev says that if she turned Dave loose on a cross-country car trip by himself she would never see him again because he doesn't know north from south, east from west, or up from down. She goes on to describe that she can be in a place she's never been before and will instantly know her directions – but not Dave, no not Dave. You see, Dave doesn't know north from south, east from west, or up from down.

Dave replies, "Right now, at this very instant, I'm supposed to be here in Chaplain's Tavern drinking margaritas with the three of you, and I am – so . . .

Who Gives A Shit."

THE ROMANTIC

    Edward takes his wife, Helen, out to dinner one night a year, just to give her a break from life's daily routine.

    Since Helen has been a little cranky lately, Edward decides that the time is right. "I don't suppose you'd like to go out to dinner tonight," he says.

    Helen, who has had over a year to think of an appropriate reply to Edward's dinner invitation says,

"Who Gives A Shit."

FISH STORY

Larry returned from his Canadian fishing trip with no fish but with photos of himself holding a string of fish so huge he could barely lift them. There's some speculation that Larry might have bought the fish at a fish market or maybe borrowed them from a real fisherman for the photo or maybe that he threw some dynamite into the lake to blast a few fish to the surface. None of that may be true, but Larry, even if you caught the fish yourself as you say ...

Who Gives A Shit.

BLOODY MARYS

Stephen, the bartender says that the special mix that they use for their Bloody Marys is a secret concoction imported from Brazil.

Who Gives A Shit.

CHICAGO, CHICAGO

    Winthrop says that he was born in Chicago, works in Chicago, lives in Chicago, plays in Chicago, and hasn't found the need to leave the city limits for thirty-eight years.

Who Gives A Shit.

SHOOTING THE SHIT

    Miriam Rodgers is a professional photographer who specializes in photographing bathrooms of hotel and motel rooms and suites that celebrities stayed in. Miriam,

Who Gives A Shit.

WHO'S COUNTING?

This book's proofreader says that this group of ten things that nobody gives a shit about actually contains eleven things that nobody gives a shit about.

Who Gives A Shit.

TWELFTH
TEN THINGS NOBODY GIVES A SHIT ABOUT

SHAPE UP

Ralph and his wife, Edna, retired at age 65 a few months ago. Some of their friends have occasionally remarked to their 43-year-old daughter, Carolyn, how wonderful it is that Ralph and Edna are having such a good time in retirement. But, the more she hears, the more Carolyn worries about them – it sounds like they are totally out of control. Finally, Carolyn decides to confront her mom and dad.

"Mom, Dad," she begins, "I have been hearing some disturbing things about your activities lately. People tell me that you're going out two or three nights a week, going to Rock 'N' Roll concerts, drinking, gambling, running with a fast crowd, and staying out well past midnight. It sounds like you're acting like a couple of teenagers – and I just wanted to hear what you have to say for yourselves."

"Carolyn, Dear," her mother says slowly, "I guess everything you say is true and all we've got to say about it is . . . we're having the time of our lives, so . . .

Who Gives A Shit."

THE AUTHOR

Well, you took an hour of my time to describe to me the highly detailed book about your life that you wrote and self-published. After hearing your story, there's only one thing that can be said.

Who Gives A Shit.

ALL SOLD OUT

The table waiter apologizes that the restaurant is all out of Rocky Mountain Oysters and artichokes this evening.

Who Gives A Shit.

PROBLEM OR SOLUTION?

Management at Axelrod Company brought in a motivational speaker, Dr. Wells, to speak to its employees in an effort to increase loyalty, effort, enthusiasm, and productivity. Dr. Wells' main theme was, "As an employee, you're one of two things - you're either part of the problem or you're part of the solution. Decide in your mind which you will be."

Whipple, who is no longer employed at Axelrod at the time of this writing, raises his hand and says, "Dr. Wells, there is a third option that you seem to have overlooked, which is . . .

Who Gives A Shit."

LOVE MACHINE

Jay Cantenelli, Lead vocalist for the Rock 'N' Roll band, "Upward," claims that in the band's forty-year career he bedded 2,486 women. Other than his wife of forty-one years,

Who Gives A Shit.

SLIP O' THE TONGUE

Ms. Madeline Madison is a prim and proper cultured lady of high moral character and great self control. That's why when she dropped the sugar bowl while serving dinner to her guests and the word, "shit" slipped from her lips, she was terribly embarrassed and apologized profusely for using such vulgar language. Madeline,

Who Gives A Shit.

IT'S CHIC, DAAHLING

Alleged actress LaRaye Lennae is being interviewed by a television entertainment reporter on the red carpet at the Academy Awards. She volunteers that she's wearing a dress created by the renowned French designer Pierre LaBlanc.

Who Gives A Shit.

EXPECTING

The tabloids are all tripping over themselves to report that alleged movie actress Samantha Smythe is pregnant.

Who Gives A Shit.

THE BABYSITTER

Shirley spent the weekend babysitting for her five-month-old grandson while her daughter and her husband took a well-deserved getaway. Shirley will tell anyone she can ambush into listening that the grandson is not only handsome but smart and talented, being able to cry in perfect pitch, and that he's charming to boot. Not only that, but he has the most beautiful blue eyes and a brilliant smile. And, he has his mother's nose and his father's ears and a full head of thick brown hair and dimples and personality and . . .

Shirley, this may not have occurred to you but when it comes to your little bundle of joy, there's nobody outside of your immediate family . . .

Who Gives A Shit.

CONVOLUTED JUSTICE

    It's true – the media is overrun with nauseating stories of alleged actress Kim Kardashian and alleged actress, Lindsay Lohan. But, that's not all bad.

    There's only room in the media for so many stories about so many people, and no more. Thus, the proliferation of stories about Kardashian and Lohan has knocked stories about Paris Hilton clean off the charts. And when considered in that light, if we have to put up with a few stories about Kardashian and Lohan . . .

Who Gives A Shit.

THIRTEENTH
TEN THINGS NOBODY GIVES A SHIT ABOUT

ROCKET SHOPPER

    Willie, who considers himself to be one of the fastest shoppers on the planet, charged into the gift shop, selected a birthday card for his wife, paid for it, and exited the store all within two minutes. Sure, the heading on the card said, "TO MY MOTHER," but since it's the thought that counts,

Who Gives A Shit.

CHILD GENIUS

    The bumper sticker on the station wagon says, "My child is a middle school honor student."

Who Gives A Shit.

RED AND GREEN ONES

Kelsey accuses her husband, Earl, of sorting out all of the red and green M & M chocolate candies from the bag and eating them, leaving the blue, yellow, and brown ones for her. Kelsey further states that the red and green ones taste better, which is why Earl took all of them.

Earl is now eating blue, yellow, and brown M & M chocolate candies for breakfast, lunch, and dinner and will be until they are all gone, all because his attempt at logic was to tell Kelsey that the red, green, blue, yellow, and brown ones all taste the same, so . . .

Who Gives A Shit.

RIGHTS

Okay, there's the Bill of Rights, Civil Rights, Animal Rights, Tenant's Rights, Gay Rights, Parental Rights, Reading you your Rights, and The Price is Right. But, since Harriet can't find Mr. Right, her attitude toward the rest of the rights is,

Who Gives A Shit.

CHUG-A-LUG

Harvey, a man of great religious faith and unbending moral principles, was shocked when he saw his church's pastor drinking a glass of beer while eating at a local pizzeria with his wife. Harvey reported this scandalous behavior to the church council who agreed to consider the matter and promised to inform Harvey of their decision.

A week later, Harvey received a letter from the church council that said, "In the matter of the pastor's drinking a glass or two of beer,

Who Gives A Shit."

THE BOSS'S WIFE

It's the annual Employee Appreciation Party designed to say "Thanks" to all of the employees for their hard work and dedication and to allow management and workers to mingle on a social level.

As the Big Boss's wife floats from one group of employees to another, she always makes it a point to inform everyone that she graduated from Vassar – or as she says it, "Vaaaaassaar."

Who Gives A Shit.

PIE, ANYONE?

Jim says that he beat our twenty-five other contestants to become the Montana State Champion by throwing a dried cow pie 137 feet.

Who Gives A Shit.

INVOLVED

Arthur Melbourne is a highly skilled actor who has won four Academy Awards and who is adored by fans all over the world. Arthur has recently started using his fame as a springboard to express his political and social viewpoints on a wide range of topics including global warming, gay marriage, animal rights, income taxes, immigration reform, legalizing marijuana, gun control, legalizing prostitution, and parking meters.

Arthur, you're one hell of an actor, but when it comes to your viewpoints on stuff you know nothing about . . .

Who Gives A Shit.

MISTER FIXERUP

The front end of Dan's car would shake and vibrate whenever he drove over fifty miles per hour, so he took the car to Mike the Mechanic. Dan described the car's problem in great detail. Mike said that he could fix it.

The next day, Dan picked up his car from Mike the Mechanic and received an itemized invoice for all of the repairs that Mike had made. Mike replaced the spark plugs, spark plug wires, distributor cap, brake pads, windshield wiper blades, and radiator coolant for a total of $495.

The following morning, Dan returned to Mike's Garage and told him that the car still shook and vibrated exactly as it did before he brought car in to have the problem fixed. Dan told Mike that he was damn mad that Mike had replaced a whole lot of stuff that he hadn't asked for but hadn't fixed the problem he brought the car in for and he asked Mike the Mechanic what he was going to do about it.

Mike the Mechanic calmly asked Dan if he had paid the invoice for all of the work he had done on the car.

"Ya, I paid your damn bill," Dan snarled.

"Well, then," Mike the Mechanic said,

"Who Gives A Shit."

PASTRY, ANYONE?

The sign on the counter at Al's Bakery says, "DOENUGHTS $1.00 EACH."

A customer, Harriet, who was the third grade spelling champion about forty years ago, feels compelled to point out to Al that he has misspelled a word on his sign. Harriet points to the sign and says, "The word *doughnut* is spelled d-o-u-g-h-n-u-t."

Al replies, "This is a bakery and people can figure out what the sign means, so . . .

Who Gives A Shit."

FOURTEENTH
TEN THINGS NOBODY GIVES A SHIT ABOUT

KINDLY PROFESSOR WANKEL

Professor Wankel provided this solution to the mathematical brainteaser that he had assigned to his Advanced Engineering Calculus class: "The inversion of the square root of the algorithm of the number 32 divided by the tangent of the sum of the numbers 73 plus 34 divided by the square root of the product of the numbers multiplied by the sine of the number 12 divided by the cosine of the number 25 divided by the coefficient of the permeable interactive function of the square root of zero divided by the random variable of the product of the free radical function of the number 168 results in the obvious answer – seven.

"For my next miracle, I'd like to read the minds of the five of you with blank looks on your faces sitting in the far back row, which is,

Who Gives A Shit."

YOUR OPINION, PLEASE

A poll on the internet asked this question: "What do you think of the First Lady's new hairstyle?" The possible answers were, (A) I like it; it looks classy, (B) I don't like it; it makes her look cheap, and (C) I'm not sure. More appropriate wording for answer (C) would have been,

(C) Who Gives A Shit.

BOWL BOUND

The matches for the college football bowl games were announced today, including a game on December 9 between Magnolia State College and Northern Kansas Tech. Our first thought is . . . "Who?" Our second thought is . . .

"Who Gives A Shit."

NO LONGER SEEING RED

The International Institute of Genetic Research says, that based on their projections, red-headed humans will be bred out of existence by the year 2125.

Who Gives A Shit.

WORKIN' LIKE A DOG

So, you say you're being overworked and underpaid, working ten- to twelve-hour days. Well, we'd like to be there when you state your case to your boss and you tell him that you're gonna quit unless you get a pay raise - just to hear him tell you . . .

"Who Gives A Shit."

WHO POPPED THE COUNTRY?

Music critics have been evaluating singer Jenna James' latest album and can't decide if it's a *country album* or a *pop album*. One critic contacted Jenna's record label for a clarification and a spokesperson said, "The album has already sold millions of copies, so to answer your question about whether the album is country or pop, it appears there's nobody in the music-buying public . . .

Who Gives A Shit."

WATCH THIS

The sign next to an expensive gold and diamond wrist watch in the window of a jewelry store says "Can withstand water pressure up to a depth of 150 feet."

Who Gives A Shit.

ABOVE THE GRASS

Herman's wife has been on his case lately, pointing out an increasing number of flaws in his behavior. "Your eyebrows are getting bushy, you spill on the front of your shirt when you eat, you run around with your shoes untied, you wear the same baggy pants and faded shirt for a week at a time, you stare at women when they walk by, and you mumble when you talk."

Herman says, "I'm eighty-five years old and still above the grass, so . . .

Who Gives A Shit."

SAY WHAT?

Karen and her husband, Louie, went to Karen's parents for dinner. After dinner, Louie and his father-in-law retired to the living room to watch television and Karen and her mother went to the kitchen to wash dishes. Karen proceeded to tell her mother what a miserable disappointment Louie was. "He earns damn near nothing at his job, he has no ambition, he is fat, dumb, and lazy, he's ugly, and he snores like a locomotive."

"I can hear you," Louie yells from the living room. Karen replies,

"Who Gives A Shit."

BREAK A LEG

Guests in the packed gymnasium for the high school graduation ceremony had already endured long and boring speeches by the school Principal, school board president, and some nitwit who is running for congress when the senior class valedictorian took the stage. To say he was ill at ease is a gross understatement as witnessed by his pale face, wobbly knees, shaking hands, blank stare, and cotton mouth. He began to speak and all that came out was "uh, uh, Grrrr, uh, uhhhh." And then, he passed out. Perhaps that was not the message of congratulations, inspiration, hope, and challenge that he had planned to deliver to his classmates, but it was short and was definitely memorable, so . . .

Who Gives A Shit.

FIFTEENTH
TEN THINGS NOBODY GIVES A SHIT ABOUT

WHO'S WHO

    Maynard, who drives a forklift at the local sawmill was thrilled when he received a letter in the mail saying that he had been selected to be included in the new edition of WHO'S WHO OF AMERICAN EXECUTIVES - and all he had to do was buy one copy of the book for $99 to be included. Upon contemplation, Maynard recalled that the closest he had ever come to being an executive was the time he snuck into the executive restroom, but somehow the WHO'S WHO people must have found out about that and figured it was enough to include him in WHO'S WHO. To show his appreciation for being included in WHO'S WHO, Maynard bought two books – one for himself and one for his mother. Maynard proudly told the guys at work that he was being included in WHO'S WHO OF AMERICAN EXECUTIVES and they all shouted in unison . . .

"Who Gives A Shit."

OOMPAH

Radio Station KPKA, devoted to playing polka music 24 hours a day, has gone off the air.

Who Gives A Shit.

MONKEYING AROUND

Carl boasts that he owns the largest collection of ceramic monkeys in the world – brown monkeys, red monkeys, white monkeys, scratching monkeys, smiling monkeys, monkeying around monkeys, climbing monkeys, drunk monkeys, laughing monkeys, monkeys that swing from ...

Who Gives A Shit.

NO ACTION

Wilfred says that he has not gone to the bathroom in five days.

Who Gives A Shit.

WHO YOU?

"Tell me about yourself," she says.

"Well," he replies, "my father is president of Nor'Easter Bank and my grandfather started Moore Manufacturing Company."

She says,

"Who Gives A Shit." and *"Who Gives A Shit."*

NO NIBBLING

Levi, who is a self-styled barroom philosopher, offered this technique for handling a mess that you have created for yourself, "When you have screwed up and have to eat shit, don't nibble." When Herbie, standing at the end of the bar, heard these words, it was an enlightening moment similar to getting hit over the head with a beer keg. Herbie vowed that in the future he would follow Levi's advice and that when he screwed up he would no longer simply say,

"Who Gives A Shit."

HAPPINESS

John was deep into his third martini when it came over him like a tidal wave – the secret to a happy and worry-free life. First, realize that about 99% of the things that a person worries about never materialize anyway. So, when faced with a problem, concern, or worry, all you have to do is take a deep breath and say the magical words and, *poof,* the problem will disappear. And, here are the magical words that you should memorize and use daily:

"Who Gives A Shit."

ETYMOLOGY

We know you have no idea what "Etymology" is, so we'll tell you – it is the study of the origin of words. After reading this far in this book, you're probably wondering, "Where did the word, *shit*, come from?" A fair question. We will provide an explanation.

Somewhere around 1835, an enterprising man named Shorty Hubers recognized the value of education, so he started a school of higher learning named *Shorty Hubers Institute of Technology*, which is a very long name, so it eventually became known by the initials, S.H.I.T.

Graduates of S.H.I.T were well versed in mathematics, astrology, language arts, geography, geology, and horsemanship. Sometimes, when engaged in a debate with someone of lesser education and knowledge, out of frustration over their adversary's lack of comprehension, a graduate of The Institute would proclaim, "You don't know SHIT," in reference to their prestigious education.

In response, the lesser educated would often hurl back,

"Who Gives A Shit."

TELLING IT LIKE IT IS

    I finally told my wife that I was writing this book and she said,

"Who Gives A Shit."

    So, I'll just stop right here.

TO OBTAIN MORE BOOKS

If you want to obtain more copies of this book, you can get them from the following:

Local Book Store:

If they do not have the books in stock, they can order them for you.

Online:

www.amazon.com
(Paperback and Kindle eBook)

www.barnesandnoble.com
(Paperback and Nook eBook)

Directly from the Publisher:

Sweet Memories Publishing
P.O. Box 497
Arnolds Park, IA 51331-0497

Your Cost: $10.00 per book plus $2.50 shipping for the first book and $.50 shipping for each additional book. Send payment with your order.

For a quote from the publisher on massive quantities of the book, email: sweetmemories@mchsi.com

And, if you don't want any more copies of this book . . .

Really, Who Gives A Shit.

YOUR TURN

Use the following pages to make a list of things that you don't give a shit about. Go ahead – it's fun and it will make you feel a whole lot better about life in general.

THINGS I DON'T GIVE A SHIT ABOUT

MORE THINGS I DON'T GIVE A SHIT ABOUT

STILL MORE THINGS I DON'T GIVE A SHIT ABOUT

YET MORE THINGS I DON'T GIVE A SHIT ABOUT

RIGHT. MORE THINGS I DON'T GIVE A SHIT ABOUT

YUP - MORE STUFF I DON'T GIVE A SHIT ABOUT

A FEW MORE THINGS I DON'T GIVE A SHIT ABOUT

THE FINAL STUFF I DON'T GIVE A SHIT ABOUT

Made in the USA
Charleston, SC
20 July 2013